❧ CONTENTS ☙

❧ INTRODUCTION ❧
by Coretta Scott King

This book is about black Americans who served society through the excellence of their achievements. It forms a part of the rich history of black men and women in America—a history of stunning accomplishments in every field of human endeavor, from literature and art to science, industry, education, diplomacy, athletics, jurisprudence, even polar exploration.

Not all of the people in this history had the same ideals, but I think you will find something that all of them had in common. Like Martin Luther King, Jr., they all decided to become "drum majors" and serve humanity. In that principle—whether it was expressed in books, inventions, or song—they found something outside themselves to use as a goal and a guide. Something that showed them a way to serve others, instead of only living for themselves.

Reading the stories of these courageous men and women not only helps us discover the principles that we will use to guide our own lives but also teaches us about our black heritage and about America itself. It is crucial for us to know the heroes and heroines of our history and to realize that the price we paid in our struggle for equality in America was dear. But we must also understand that we have gotten as far as we have partly because America's democratic system and ideals made it possible.

We are still struggling with racism and prejudice. But the great men and women in this series are a tribute to the spirit of our democratic ideals and the system in which they have flourished. And that makes their stories special and worth knowing.

❦ PROFILES OF GREAT ❦

BLACK AMERICANS

Pioneers of Discovery

❦❦

Edited by Richard Rennert

Introduction by Coretta Scott King

Ⅲ A Chelsea House
Ⅲ Multibiography

Chelsea House Publishers
New York   Philadelphia

Copyright © 1994 by Chelsea House Publishers, a division of
Main Line Book Co. All rights reserved. Printed and bound in
the United States of America.

First Printing

1 3 5 7 9 8 6 4 2

Library of Congress Cataloging-in-Publication Data

  Pioneers of discovery/edited by Richard Rennert.
  p. cm.—(Profiles of great black Americans) (A Chelsea House
multibiography)
  Includes bibliographical references and index.
Summary: Short biographies of eight American pioneers of
discovery, including Benjamin Banneker, George Washington
Carver, and Lewis Latimer.
  ISBN   0-7910-2067-3.
          0-7910-2068-1 (pbk.)
      1. Afro-American scientists—Biography—Juvenile literature.
2. Discoveries in science—United States—History—Juvenile
literature. [1. Scientists. 2. Afro-Americans—Biography.]
I. Rennert, Richard Scott, 1956–   . II. Series. III. Series: A
Chelsea House multibiography.
93-14423   Q141.P49 1993
509.2'273—dc20   CIP
[B]   AC

BENJAMIN BANNEKER

Astronomer and mathematician Benjamin Banneker was born on November 9, 1731, in what was then the British colony of Maryland. His father was a former slave, born in Africa, who had bought his freedom. Benjamin's mother was the daughter of a white Englishwoman, Molly Welsh, and a freed African slave.

In 1682 Molly Welsh had been falsely accused of stealing milk on the farm in England where she worked as a dairy maid. She was put on trial and convicted, and as her punishment she was deported to the English colonies in North America. In 1683 Welsh settled on a farm in Maryland as an indentured servant, a person who was legally bound to work for an employer for a certain number of years.

Welsh's term of servitude was seven years. When she received her freedom in 1690, she rented a small plot of land and grew tobacco. After several years she had made enough money from the sale of her crop to buy a small patch of land near the Patapsco River. A few years later Welsh bought two slaves to help her farm the land. One of the slaves, named Bannaka, told Welsh that he had been a prince in Africa. This may have been true, because during this time, rival African states at war often captured the opposing tribe's royal family and sold them to European slave traders.

Bannaka was said to be "a man of bright intelligence, fine temper, with a very agreeable presence, dignified manners, and contemplative habits." He held pride in his African heritage, maintaining his faith while other slaves converted to Christianity. He also kept his African name, although it was changed slightly.

By 1696 Welsh had freed both of her slaves. About this time she married Bannaka, and the couple took the surname of Banneky. They operated a prosperous tobacco farm and eventually had four children, all of whom worked on the farm. The oldest, Mary, married a freed slave named Robert from a neighboring farm in 1730. Their first child, Benjamin, was born a year later. The couple took Mary's surname, which was later changed to Banneker.

Throughout his childhood Benjamin and his three younger sisters worked on the family farm. They helped with the household chores and sowed the tobacco seeds. Although tobacco farming took up most of Benjamin's time, he did not like it very much. Whenever he was able to take a break from farm work, he read. His grandmother Molly Welsh taught him how to read and write and to perform simple arithmetic. She also arranged for him to attend classes for several years at a local Quaker school, and his interest in mathematics and science grew. He enjoyed calculating mathematical problems and figuring out statistics.

At the age of 21, Banneker decided to build a clock, even though he did not know how one worked. Mechanical timepieces were rare in colonial America, but Banneker managed to borrow a pocket watch to use as a model. He took the watch apart and made drawings of its interior to teach himself how it worked. He then reproduced the watch parts by carving them from wood, making them considerably bigger, and assembled them into a large clock. He even added a bell, so that the clock chimed on the hour. Neighbors often came to see it, and Banneker himself became celebrated locally for his mathematical ability.

In 1759, following the death of his father, Banneker became responsible for running the family tobacco farm. During the next 20 years he spent most of his time doing farm work; for relaxation he bought a flute and violin and learned to play both instruments. He liked to sit on the porch and play music in the evening. Being a free black, Banneker led a lonely life. He did not have many friends, and he never married. However, neighbors did visit to have him help make mathematical computations on deeds and other things.

In the 1780s Banneker became acquainted with the Ellicotts, a white Quaker family who lived nearby. One of the family's sons, George Ellicott, was a surveyor, and when he learned of Banneker's interest in mathematics and mechanics, he lent Banneker a telescope, drafting instruments, and several books on surveying and astronomy. Using all these materials, Banneker proceeded to teach himself both surveying and astronomy.

Soon Banneker was able to predict when eclipses of the sun and moon would occur. (An eclipse of the sun, or solar eclipse means that moonlight is blocked by the passage of earth between the moon and the sun.) Banneker also calculated a table showing the locations of celestial bodies—the sun, moon, stars, and planets—at different times of the year. Such a table is called an ephemeris; the plural is *ephemerides*.

In 1791 a cousin of George Ellicott's, Andrew Ellicott, became the chief surveyor of the nearby federal territory. A new national capital was being created on this land that later became Washington, D.C. Andrew Ellicott, hearing of Banneker's skills, invited him to help with the survey.

Several months later, after finishing this work, Banneker returned to his farm and calculated an ephemeris for the following year. In August of 1791 Banneker sent a copy of his ephemeris to Thomas Jefferson, who was then Secretary of State. Along with the calculations he enclosed a letter that complained about the "abuse and censure" of African Americans by whites, and he criticized Jefferson for not opposing slavery. In his letter, Banneker compared the enslavement of blacks to the way in which England had treated the American colonies before the colonies declared their independence.

Jefferson wrote back to Banneker, acknowledging the receipt of his letter and calculations. The future president, who was also an amateur scientist, then sent Banneker's calculations to an acquaintance, the head of the French Academy of Sciences in Paris. Jefferson's and Banneker's letters were later published in pamphlet form and received wide publicity.

In December 1791 Banneker published his ephemeris as part of an almanac entitled *Benjamin Banneker's Pennsylvania, Delaware, Maryland and Virginia Almanack and Ephemeris, for the Year of Our Lord, 1792; Being Bissextile, or Leap-Year, and the Sixteenth Year of American Independence, Which Commenced July 4, 1776.* In addition to the ephemeris, the almanac included several essays on scientific topics.

The publication of Banneker's almanac was sponsored by several abolitionist societies—groups of men and women who worked for the abolition of slavery. At that time many people who supported slavery believed that Africans were not as intelligent as people of European ancestry. Abolitionists used Banneker's work to show that blacks had abilities equal to those of whites.

The first edition of the almanac sold out quickly, and a second edition was printed. The book's widespread popularity freed Banneker from heavy farm work. Instead of raising cash crops, he kept only a small home garden and raised bees. This gave him more time to continue his calculations and to chat with the many visitors who flocked to his cabin, for Banneker had become a celebrity.

Banneker published a new *Almanack and Ephemeris* each year for several years. The *Almanack* for 1793 included copies of Banneker's letter to Jefferson and Jefferson's response. The last known issue of Banneker's *Almanack and Ephemeris* appeared in 1797, probably because support for the antislavery movement was then declining. However, Banneker continued to prepare an ephemeris for each year until 1804. He also published a book about bees and calculated the life cycle of the seventeen-year locust.

One of Banneker's closest friends in his later years was Susanna Mason, a cousin of the Ellicotts. Mason was the founder of an association for the relief of the poor in Baltimore. She met Banneker in 1796, and the two wrote letters to one another. Mason wrote a poem in one of these letters:

But thou, a man exalted high,
Conspicuous in the world's keen eye

On record now thy name's enrolled
And future ages will be told,
There lived a man called Banneker,
An African Astronomer.

Banneker died at his cabin on October 9, 1806, one month before his 75th birthday. He had left many of his personal effects, including his journals and scientific instruments, to George Ellicott, and these were quickly carted away. Banneker's funeral service was held on his farm two days after his death. As the body was being buried, his cabin nearby burst into flames and burned to the ground. Everything remaining in the structure was destroyed—including the famous clock that he had built many years before.

| JAMES BECKWOURTH |

Frontiersman James Pierson Beckwourth was born in Frederick County, Virginia, around the year 1800. His father was Jennings Beckwith, a member of a prominent landholding family in Virginia. James's mother was probably a light-skinned slave on the Beckwith plantation. After Beckwith's legal wife died in 1808, Beckwith, his son James, and James's mother moved west to a farm near St. Charles, Missouri, to start a new life.

Although James was legally a slave, his father treated him kindly. When James was 10, Jennings Beckwith sent him to school in St. Louis, where he learned to read and write. When he was not attending school, James loved to be outdoors with his father, traipsing through the acres of wilderness surrounding their home.

About 1819 James was apprenticed to a pair of blacksmiths in the city. However, James was more interested in his social life than the daily drudgery of blacksmithing. He frequently got into arguments with his employers over his behavior. One day, in the midst of an angry dispute, a passing constable tried to intervene. James Beckwourth knocked out the policeman and fled the scene.

After several days in hiding, Beckwourth returned to his father, who arranged for his release from the apprenticeship. At this time Jennings Beckwith decided that it was time to free his son, and he went to court to sign papers that formally released Beckwourth from slavery. For several years James Beckwourth worked on the family farm. In the early 1820s he traveled up the Mississippi River to Fever River, Illinois (later renamed Galena), to work in the nearby lead mines.

During these years Beckwourth's love of the wilderness had increased, and he began to dream of a life of solitude and freedom as a trapper and trader on the western frontier. That opportunity came in

1823, when he joined a fur-trapping expedition sponsored by two entrepreneurs named William Ashley and Andrew Henry. Ashley and Henry's venture later became the Rocky Mountain Fur Company.

Beckwourth's activities during the next few years are not known in detail, although he presumably lived as a "mountain man," as frontiersmen were known, hunting and trapping. In June 1825 he attended a gathering of more than 100 American trappers at Henry's Fork, a settlement on the Green River in the Rocky Mountains. For the next 15 years these "conventions," or rendezvous, of mountain men became annual events at different prearranged locations throughout the Rockies. During several days of revelry at Henry's Fork in 1825, Beckwourth established what became a lifelong reputation as a talented raconteur, or storyteller.

Like all successful trappers, James Beckwourth was well-versed in the habits and customs of Native American tribes in the West, and many Indians respected him for his prowess. In fact, friendly Indians could be especially helpful to trappers because they often knew the best sources of game. Not long after attending the 1828 rendezvous of mountain men, Beckwourth and his close friend, the celebrated frontiersman Jim Bridger, were trapping beaver one day near the Powder River when they encountered a party of Crow Indians. Beckwourth knew of his favorable reputation among the Crows, who were generally friendly to white men, and he allowed himself to be "captured" by them. The curious and delighted Crows took Beckwourth back to their camp.

During the next eight years Beckwourth lived with the Crows in the region of what is now Montana and Wyoming while he continued his life as a fur trapper and trader with a new employer, the American Fur Company. The Indians believed that Beckwourth himself was part Crow, an impression that he did not correct. Beckwourth enjoyed the relative freedom of Native American society and took many Indian wives over the years. He engaged in the common Crow practice of stealing horses from white men and earned the nickname Enemy of Horses. Beckwourth earned another nickname, Bloody Arm, for his frequent participation in Crow war parties.

The American Fur Company terminated Beckwourth's employment with them in 1836, and shortly afterward he left the Crows and drifted back to St. Louis. He remained there for several months with little to occupy his time except heavy drinking and street fights. In 1837 Senator Thomas Hart Benton of Missouri called for the formation of a brigade of experienced volunteers to fight the Seminole Indians in Florida. Beckwourth promptly joined up and served in the brigade as a mule skinner and messenger.

Eager to get back to the mountaineering life he preferred, Beckwourth returned to St. Louis in the summer of 1838. After several days in the city he headed west with two male companions to resume his work as a fur trader. This time he was after buffalo skins, and during the next few years he established a flourishing business in Colorado and New Mexico by trading whiskey to the Cheyenne Indians for the skins.

In the early 1840s he established a general store in Taos, New Mexico, and married a woman named Luisa Sandoval. In the fall of 1842 Beckwourth and his wife set up a trading post in south-central Colorado that soon became the settlement of Pueblo. Not long afterward, Beckwourth left to head a trading expedition to southern California, abandoning his wife and their infant daughter in Pueblo.

Beckwourth arrived in California just in time to participate in the Bear Flag Rebellion, an uprising of mountain men who were trying to free California from Mexican rule. During the uprising he stole 2,000 horses from several Mexican-owned ranches near Los Angeles and drove them back to Pueblo, where he sold them. With the proceeds, Beckwourth bought a hotel and saloon in Santa Fe, New Mexico, which he ran successfully for several years. When war broke out between Mexico and the United States in 1846, Beckwourth volunteered as an army messenger, carrying communications between Santa Fe and Fort Leavenworth, Kansas, on horseback.

In the late summer of 1848 Beckwourth moved back to California and became a mail courier for the government, riding a regular route nearly 200 miles long between Monterey and Dana's Ranch, the site of present-day Santa Maria. By 1849 Beckwourth had resigned this job and become a familiar figure in the gold-mining camps of northern California, earning his living by playing cards and occasionally prospecting.

Soon Beckwourth had resumed his familiar occupation as a horse "trader." His horse-stealing and selling activities took him into the valley of the Sierra Nevada, the mountain range lying along the eastern border of California. Sometime during the winter of 1850 he discovered a pass through the mountains that was later named the Beckwourth Trail.

Eventually thousands of pioneers would follow the Beckwourth Trail to California, which had become a state following its cession to the United States by Mexico in 1848.

Beckwourth established a combination ranch, trading post, and hotel along the trail that became famous as the Beckwourth Ranch. Nicknamed the emigrants' landing place, the ranch provided food and lodging to many new settlers. Even those who had no money to pay were welcomed by their gracious host, who entertained his guests with many stories of his adventures as a mountain man.

During the winter of 1854 Beckwourth dictated his life story to a guest at the ranch named T. D. Bonner, a would-be poet and journalist from Massachusetts. Bonner turned Beckwourth's tales into a book, *The Life and Adventures of James P. Beckwourth, Mountaineer, Scout, Pioneer, and Chief of the Crow Nation*, which was published in 1856 by Harper Brothers in New York City following Bonner's return to the East Coast. Although Beckwourth made no money from the sale of the book—Bonner pocketed all the royalties and then disappeared—he did become something of a celebrity, and many visitors came to the ranch to catch a glimpse of him.

In 1858 the footloose Beckwourth abandoned the ranch and traveled for a while as far east as St. Louis. He then settled in Denver, where he opened a general store that became a frequent stopping place for Cheyenne Indians. Beckwourth became an outspoken defender of the rights of the Cheyenne, who were being displaced from their lands by new white settlers from the East. Beckwourth's friendly relations with the Indians ended in the fall of 1864, however, when he was forced by U.S. Army troops to lead them to an encampment of Cheyenne and Arapaho at Sand Creek, Colorado. The troops massacred most of the Indians, and the survivors blamed Beckwourth for betraying them, although he claimed that he would have been hanged had he not cooperated with the troops.

The details of Beckwourth's last years are not known. He apparently worked for a while as a scout and dispatch rider at Fort Laramie, Wyoming. Sometime in 1866 he began a new trading venture with his old friend Jim Bridger. He died in October 1866 while visiting a tribe of Crow Indians along the Bighorn River.

GUION BLUFORD

Aerospace engineer and astronaut Guion Stewart Bluford, Jr., was born in Philadelphia, Pennsylvania, on November 22, 1942, the oldest of three brothers. His mother taught special education classes in the Philadelphia public schools, and his father was a mechanical engineer. As a child Guion—pronounced Guy-on—was nicknamed Guy.

Guy Bluford collected numerous mechanical toys which he enjoyed taking apart and putting back together. He was especially interested in flying, and he built model airplanes and collected pictures of planes. He also liked to study the flight of other objects, including table tennis balls and the folded newspapers he delivered every day. Bluford decided at an early age that he wanted to build planes when he grew up.

Bluford was raised in an integrated Philadelphia neighborhood and attended integrated schools, and his parents taught him and his brothers that they were capable of accomplishing anything they wished, provided they worked hard enough. During the early 1950s scientists in both the United States and the Soviet Union were working on artificial earth satellites, spacecraft that would be launched into orbit around the earth to gather information on space. The goal of scientists in both countries was to eventually send human beings into space to explore the universe. Bluford, who was then in junior high school, was excited by stories of space exploration and began to focus seriously on a career as an aerospace engineer, a person who works on the design, construction, and operation of spacecraft.

In the fall of 1957, shortly before Guy Bluford's 15th birthday, the Soviet Union launched the satellite *Sputnik I*, ushering in the space age. The United States immediately stepped up its space program and in 1958 created NASA, the National Aeronautics and Space Administration. The government also encouraged renewed interest in mathematics and the sciences in the nation's schools in order to catch up with the Soviets. Bluford eagerly followed newspaper and television accounts of missile launches by NASA in Cape Canaveral, Florida, but in the high school he attended no one seemed especially interested in the space race.

At Overbrook High School, Bluford was an average student, and his guidance counselors did not encourage his interest in aerospace engineering or even in attending college. Instead, they advised him to enroll in a technical school after graduation and learn a mechanical trade. Both Bluford and his parents ignored the advice of the counselors, who seemed unaware of the fact that several generations of family members had attended college and in many instances earned advanced degrees. In the fall of 1960 Bluford enrolled in the aerospace engineering program at Pennsylvania State University.

For the first time, Bluford later recalled, he began to realize that he was different because he was black. There were relatively few African American students at Penn State, and some of them were active participants in the civil rights movement that had begun in the late 1950s. While Bluford supported the movement, he concentrated on his education, which included numerous courses in math and science. When both the Soviet Union and the United States launched men into space in 1961, the spring of his freshman year, Bluford had an even greater incentive to remain focused on his goal of building spacecraft.

During his four years at Penn State, Bluford was a member of the air force ROTC (Reserve Officers' Training Corps). He decided in his senior year that he would become an air force pilot to fulfill his required military service obligation. Bluford graduated from Penn State in 1964 and received the ROTC's Distinguished Graduate Award. He had married a fellow student during his last year at college, and shortly after graduation their first son, Guion III, was born.

With his wife and son, Bluford moved to Arizona for pilot training at Williams Air Force Base. He received his pilot wings in 1965, the same year that his second son, James Trevor, was born. Bluford had little time to spend with his family, however. The United States was engaged in the Vietnam War, and during the next few years Bluford flew 144 combat missions in Southeast Asia, piloting an F-4C Phantom jet. He logged 3,000 hours of flying time and received 10 air force medals for competence and bravery.

After Bluford returned to the United States, the air force sent him to teach cross-country and acrobatic flying at Sheppard Air Force Base in Texas, where he accumulated 1,300 hours of instructing. Bluford still hoped to become an aerospace engineer, and he applied to the Air Force Institute of Technology for further training. Despite stiff competition, he was accepted in 1972 and graduated two years later, receiving a master's degree with distinction.

Bluford continued graduate studies in aerospace engineering at the Institute during the next four years while he worked at the Air Force Flight Dynamics Laboratory at Wright-Patterson Air Force Base in Ohio. In 1978 he received a Ph.D. in aerospace engineering with a minor in laser physics, the study of light and energy. As part of his requirements for the doctorate, Bluford developed a computer program that could calculate the pressure, density, and velocity of the air surrounding the wings of a plane as it moved through space.

About the time he received his doctorate, Bluford applied for the U.S. astronaut program, under the direction of NASA. He believed that NASA was the best place to learn about the latest developments in aerospace technology, and as an astronaut he could combine his interests in flying and engineering. Several weeks after submitting his application Bluford was notified of his selection as an astronaut candidate and invited to work at the NASA-sponsored Johnson Space Center in Houston, Texas. In 1978 nearly 9,000 other Americans applied for the astronaut program; Bluford was one of only 35 men and women chosen that year.

Bluford moved his family to Houston and began a year of training. Upon his completion in 1979 he was officially made an astronaut and during the next few years learned how to fly a space shuttle. NASA had first begun developing space shuttles in 1972. Part rocket, part spacecraft, and part airplane, shuttles were designed to carry human beings out into space for exploration and scientific investigation. Other uses were developed for shuttles, including the launching of communications satellites and the creation of space stations. Shuttles are propelled by rockets and have wings like airplanes so that they can glide on air currents. Like airplanes—but unlike most rockets—they can also navigate in outer space.

The first space shuttle, *Columbia*, was launched in April 1981. During the following year it made three more flights. In the spring of 1983 the second space shuttle, *Challenger*, was launched. Bluford was selected to fly on *Challenger*'s third flight, scheduled for that summer. Although Bluford was not the first black man to be selected for the astronaut program, he would make history as the first black American in space.

In the early morning darkness of August 30, 1983, Lieutenant Colonel Guion Bluford, Jr., was one of five astronauts aboard the *Challenger* as it rose from the launchpad at Cape Canaveral and moved into orbit around the earth. As a mission specialist, Bluford experimented with the Canadian-built remote manipulator arm during *Challenger*'s six-day flight. He also had chief responsibility for one of the major goals of the mission: the deployment of a communications satellite sponsored by the Indian government.

Bluford made the first nighttime launch and landing in the history of the shuttle program. His second flight was aboard the Mission 61-A/Spacelab D1 in

October and November 1985. Bluford was one of eight people on this scientific mission. Upon landing, he had logged 314 hours in space.

Since his historic flight on the *Challenger*, Bluford has continued to work as an aerospace engineer at the Johnson Space Center. In 1987 he earned a master's degree in business administration from the University of Houston. Bluford has received numerous awards for his achievements, including several honorary degrees from American universities, and has published several scientific papers. Bluford lives in Clear Lake, Texas, with his wife and two sons.

GEORGE WASHINGTON CARVER

Botanist George Washington Carver was born into slavery around 1864 on a farm near Diamond Grove, Missouri, owned by a white man named Moses Carver. When George was only a few weeks old, slave raiders from Arkansas attacked the farm and carried off George and his mother. Moses Carver was able to rush George's brother, Jim, to safety, but could not save the others. Moses

Carver negotiated with the raiders and swapped a racehorse for the infant's return. His mother was never found.

George took the surname of Moses Carver and grew up with the Carver family. Since the Carvers had no children, the couple raised George and his brother as their own. He was no longer a slave—slavery had been legally banned in 1865 by the Thirteenth Amendment to the U.S. Constitution—but he worked on the farm throughout his childhood. Because George was often sick, his duties were limited to doing work around the house, such as cooking and tending the family garden. When he was not helping with the housework, he explored all aspects of nature. "I literally lived in the woods," he said. "I wanted to know every strange stone, flower, insect, bird, or beast."

In his early teens he left Diamond Grove to get a formal education, since there were no schools for blacks near his home.

For several years Carver worked at odd jobs while he attended grade schools for African Americans in Kansas and in other Missouri communities. He eventually completed high school in Minneapolis, Kansas, where he had taken the middle name Washington to distinguish himself from another George Carver in the class. In 1885, he applied by mail to Highland College, a small school in Highland, Kansas. He was accepted, but when he went to register for classes and school officials saw that he was black, he was turned away. Carver was disappointed and decided to put off continuing his education for a few years.

For a while Carver homesteaded on the Kansas plains. His health was frail, however, and the work proved too hard for a lone man. In the late 1880s he moved to Iowa and eventually gained admission to Simpson College in Indianola, a small school operated by the Methodist church. Although Carver was the only African American enrolled at the school, he was treated kindly by his teachers and fellow students. "The students are wonderfully good. . . . I have the name unjustly of having one of the broadest minds in school," he said. Carver supported himself by doing laundry as well as intricate needlework—tatting, knitting, and embroidery. At Simpson he developed his aptitude for painting and for a while considered becoming an artist.

Carver's teachers, however, encouraged him to consider a more practical career, out of concern that a black man might not be able to earn a living as an artist. Carver showed a strong interest in plants and often painted flowers, so botany and agriculture seemed a logical choice. Carver himself believed that he had a responsibility to improve the lives of other black men and women, and helping them to grow better crops seemed one way of accomplishing this goal.

In 1891, following the recommendations of several teachers, Carver transferred to the Iowa State College of Agriculture (now Iowa State University), in Ames. Carver had trouble adjusting to his new college—unlike those at Simpson, the students did not all make him feel welcome. However, he soon became involved in all aspects of college life—he made new friends and joined many campus activities. Carver participated in the campus debate club, the German club, and the art club, organized an agricultural society, became the first trainer and masseur for the football team, served as missionary chairman of the Young Men's Christian Association, and joined the National Guard Student Battalion, in which he was made captain, the highest student rank. Academically, his abilities were quickly recognized by the faculty; he worked as an assistant to several professors and was eventually put in charge of the college greenhouse, where he conducted experiments in plant fertilization.

Carver received bachelor's and master's degrees in science from Iowa State. He could have remained at the college as a faculty member, but he believed even more strongly that he had to help his fellow blacks. The opportunity he was looking for came in 1896, when he was invited by the famous African American educator Booker T. Washington to become director of agricultural work at the Tuskegee Institute. Washington had founded Tuskegee in 1881 as a center for the education of African Americans, who had very few opportunities for learning.

From the moment he arrived at Tuskegee, Carver used every opportunity to make himself useful. He even played the piano in concerts to raise funds for the school. In addition to his regular teaching duties, he began a series of conferences at Tuskegee to teach African American farmers better agricultural methods. He also taught them nutrition and the importance of eating healthful foods.

Carver set up farm demonstration programs, including the training of extension agents—men who visited farmers and advised them on how to increase crop yields, prevent erosion, and control pests. To carry his program to outlying areas, Carver created what he called a movable school of agriculture. Teachers and equipment traveled in wagons to remote rural areas to give lessons in agricultural methods, nutrition, and home economics. Carver's concept of a movable school was later adopted in underdeveloped areas around the world.

Carver was shy and hardworking, and he had little concern for pleasure, personal comfort, or financial success. He was very religious, and though he often suffered from the consequences of segregation, he refused to give up his goal of promoting human welfare. He became increasingly convinced that the problems experienced by southern farmers—both black and white—were the result of several factors. Most important was the fact that they did not diversify their crops. Instead, they grew the same plant, cotton, year after year, which depleted the soil of essential minerals and attracted a specific pest, the boll weevil. Farmers also neglected soil conservation and did not know how to protect their plants against the ravages of pests.

To counter these problems, Carver launched a campaign to persuade farmers to grow other crops, including peanuts, sweet potatoes, and cowpeas. In order to do so, he knew that he had to create a demand for them. Farmers had concentrated on growing cotton because it had many commercial uses. Peanuts, sweet potatoes, and cowpeas were then grown by farmers only in their own home gardens, as food to feed their own families.

In his crude laboratory, which he had assembled from cast-off materials he found in trash piles, Carver began to develop new products from these crops. During his lifetime he introduced 325 different peanut derivatives, ranging from beverages to ink to synthetic rubber, using all parts of the plant, including the shells. In addition, he discovered more than 100 uses for sweet potatoes and made many other new products from cowpeas, soybeans, pecans, and other plants.

In his laboratory Carver made pioneering studies of crop disease and found ways to make plants resistant to attack. He also experimented with various inexpensive ways to replenish worn-out farmland. He concluded that the best method was the cheapest— recycling discarded plant material by turning it into compost and working it back into the land. Carver taught farmers that the debris they had hauled away and burned for generations was in fact a valuable resource.

Carver's numerous contributions to agriculture ultimately benefited the entire South. He was widely hailed as both a scientist and a humanitarian and given many honors, including membership in the Royal Society of London. Carver received many offers from business leaders to work for them at enormous salaries, but he always refused. Any financial rewards for his various discoveries were turned over to the Tuskegee Institute. Instead of publishing accounts of these discoveries in scientific journals, he wrote about their practical applications in numerous agricultural bulletins for farmers and housewives.

Carver remained at Tuskegee for 47 years, working and writing until shortly before his death on January 5, 1943. Eight years later his birthplace near Diamond Grove, Missouri, was proclaimed a national monument by the U.S. government.

| CHARLES DREW |

$\mathbf{P}$hysician Charles R. Drew was born in Washington, D.C., on June 3, 1904, the eldest of five children. His father was a carpet layer for a furniture company. Charles's mother, a graduate of Howard University and a former schoolteacher, stayed home to raise her children at the insistence of her husband. The Drews were a close-knit family and had strong ties to the racially integrated neighborhood of Washington in which they lived.

Charles Drew attended the local elementary school and went on to Dunbar High School, then one of the best secondary schools for African Americans in the United States. At Dunbar, Drew was an excellent student and an outstanding athlete, and upon graduating in 1922 he was awarded a partial scholarship to Amherst College in Massachusetts. Drew enrolled at Amherst that fall, augmenting his scholarship by working as a waiter. He became one of the college's leading athletes, excelling in both track and football, and paid close attention to his studies with the goal of becoming a doctor.

After graduating from Amherst in 1926, Drew needed to earn money to attend medical school. He took a job as a science instructor and athletic director at Morgan College (now Morgan State University) in Baltimore, Maryland, and worked during the summer as a swimming pool manager. By 1928 he had saved enough money to enroll at McGill University in Montreal, Canada. Drew's savings were supplemented by a loan from several of his Amherst classmates, and he also worked again as a waiter to earn extra money.

In addition to his medical studies at McGill, Drew found time for athletics. He joined the university track team and became its captain. Drew became one of Canada's top hurdlers and led McGill to several national championships. He eventually became Canada's all-time leading scorer in intercollegiate track competition.

Drew was an outstanding medical student and graduated near the top of his class in 1933, receiving both M.D. and C.M. (master of surgery) degrees. He then served a year each as intern and resident at Montreal General Hospital, where he specialized in surgery, blood typing, and problems of transfusion and blood storage.

In 1935 Drew returned to Washington and became an instructor in pathology at Howard Medical College. The following year he became resident and instructor in surgery at Freedmen's Hospital, the teaching hospital at Howard, where he continued his research in blood storage. In 1938 Drew received a grant from the Rockefeller Foundation that allowed him to serve a two-year residency in surgery at Columbia Presbyterian Hospital, which is affiliated with Columbia University in New York City.

At Columbia, Drew became the first black American to work toward the advanced degree of doctor of science in medicine. He was assigned to work under Dr. John Scudder, who was doing research in blood chemistry and transfusion.

In 1939, as part of his work at Columbia Presbyterian, Drew established a blood bank, a facility for storing donated blood that could then be transfused to hospital patients. Only two years earlier the first blood-storage facility in the United States had been established at Cook County Hospital in Chicago. When the Columbia blood bank opened in August, Drew became its director.

The previous spring, during a trip to a medical convention at the Tuskegee Institute in Alabama, Drew had stayed overnight with friends in Atlanta. There he met Lenore Robbins, a home economics teacher at Spelman College, the first school of higher education for black women in the United States. In September 1939 the couple were married and then settled in New York City, where Drew continued his graduate work at Columbia. Lenore Drew soon became her husband's research assistant.

Drew's special interest was the preservation and storage of blood. While whole blood could be preserved for up to several weeks if it was stored at a low temperature, its quality deteriorated considerably as red blood cells broke down. Drew carried out research on the use of plasma—the liquid that remained after the solids in the blood had been removed—as a substitute for whole blood in transfusions.

A little more than 50 percent of blood is composed of plasma, which contains nutrients, proteins, antibodies, and hormones. Red blood cells are the only components of blood that break down after a week of storage—and there are no red blood cells in plasma. In early 1940 Drew and Scudder began investigating the possibility of using blood plasma in place of whole blood. Their research was speeded up by pleas from the French government, which was then fighting the Germans in the early days of the Second World War. France asked the United States for help in establishing a blood bank program for its wounded soldiers.

Drew knew that plasma could be kept for as long as a month without being refrigerated. He had also determined that plasma could be dried, then reconstituted as needed by adding sterile distilled water. However, drying plasma was a complex and expensive procedure, and Drew was investigating the possibility of freezing plasma for later use. In the meantime, plans were made to begin shipments of liquid plasma to the French, but before the plan could be put into effect, France fell to the Germans in June and the project was abandoned.

That same month, Drew received his doctor of science degree from Columbia. His dissertation, "Banked Blood: A Study in Blood Preservation," was termed a masterpiece by Scudder and other professors at the medical school. Shortly after graduation, Drew returned to Washington, D.C., where he became a surgeon at Freedmen's Hospital and an assistant professor of surgery at Howard University. However, that fall he came back to New York City to direct Blood for Britain, a blood-collection program to help English war casualties. Using the procedures he had developed for the abandoned French program, Drew arranged for shipments of plasma to be sent to Great Britain for use in transfusions.

The Blood for Britain program ran successfully for five months. After it ended early in 1941 Drew joined the American Red Cross as the coordinator of a blood-banking program for the entire United States. He resigned several months later, after the U.S. War Department called for the segregation of "white" and "black" blood. He said that the War Department's decision was "indefensible" and that "there is no scientific basis for the separation of the bloods of different races." Drew returned to Howard, where he became professor of surgery and chief surgeon at Freedmen's Hospital.

The decade of the 1940s was a period of impressive accomplishments for Drew, who made major contributions to the field of medical education. More than half of the nation's black surgeons who were certified by the American Board of Surgery during the 1940s had studied under Drew at Howard. In 1947 Drew also launched a campaign to open membership in the American Medical Association, the nation's leading professional organization for physicians, to black doctors. Throughout its history the AMA had banned blacks from membership. The AMA refused to change its policies during Drew's lifetime, despite his appeals, and though he published many articles in the AMA's prestigious journal, he was never admitted as a member of the association.

Drew received several awards for his work as a physician and educator, including the Spingarn Medal, presented annually by the NAACP (National Association for the Advancement of Colored People) to an outstanding black American. In addition to his duties at Howard Medical College and the Freedmen's Hospital, Drew served on the boards of the American Cancer Society, the National Polio Foundation, and the National Society for Crippled Children, and also did volunteer work for the YMCA.

He also found time to be a concerned parent to his four young children.

Drew died suddenly on April 1, 1950, in a car accident near Haw River, North Carolina, while traveling to a meeting at the Tuskegee Institute. In the years following his death, Drew's pioneering work in human plasma research, which paved the way for later discoveries of other important uses for blood products, has been widely acknowledged. Many schools and hospitals have been named after him, and in 1976 the Charles R. Drew Commemorative Medal was established to honor exceptional achievements in the advancement of the medical education of black Americans and other minorities. Five years later the U.S. Postal Service issued a commemorative stamp in honor of Drew's contributions to science.

MATTHEW HENSON

Explorer Matthew Henson was born on August 8, 1866, on his parents' farm in Charles County, Maryland. Both of his parents had spent their entire lives as free blacks in the South. In the aftermath of the Civil War, blacks were increasingly terrorized by white supremacist groups, including the Ku Klux Klan. To escape the violence erupting around them, the family sold their farm a year after

Matthew's birth and moved to a poor section of Washington, D.C.

When Matthew was seven his mother died, and his father sent him to live with an uncle who lived nearby. Matthew attended public school for six years, and as he grew older he worked during the summer at a restaurant washing dishes. By the time he turned 13, his father had died and his uncle could no longer care for him. Matthew Henson became a full-time dishwasher and waiter at the restaurant, whose owner let him sleep in the kitchen.

After several months, Henson grew tired of his job. He heard stories of adventure from sailors who frequented the restaurant, and he decided to try for a job as a seaman. In the fall of 1879 he set out on foot for Baltimore, some 40 miles to the north of Washington, and went straight to the harbor. He was soon hired as a cabin boy on a merchant ship called the *Katie Hines*.

For the next five years Henson sailed to ports around the world, performing a variety of duties that ranged from peeling potatoes to mopping the decks. The captain took a special interest in Henson and gave him lessons in history and geography as well as training in carpentry, mechanics, first aid, and other practical subjects.

Following the captain's death, Henson left the *Katie Hines* in 1884. He worked briefly on another ship, then spent the next three years traveling around the eastern United States. By 1887 he had returned to Washington, where he became a clerk in a hat store.

One day in the spring of 1887 a naval officer named Robert Peary came into the store to buy a sun helmet. Peary was about to lead a surveying expedition to Nicaragua, where he hoped to discover a suitable route through the Central American jungle for a proposed canal to link the Atlantic and Pacific oceans. Peary needed a servant to accompany him on the expedition, and on the spur of the moment he hired the clerk who had waited on him—Matthew Henson.

During the yearlong expedition, Henson proved himself to be an invaluable aide to Peary. As part of his duties, he supervised the building of Peary's headquarters in Nicaragua and looked after the lieutenant's personal needs. Peary was so impressed by Henson that he promoted him to a position on the surveying team, where Henson earned high praise from the other crew members.

During the Nicaraguan expedition Henson continued to acquire useful skills, and he became an expert at shooting a rifle and paddling a canoe. On the voyage home, Peary told Henson that he was planning an expedition to Greenland to map unexplored areas of the Arctic. At that time no European or American explorers had gotten within 600 miles of the North Pole, and Peary secretly hoped that he would be the first to reach it. When Peary invited Henson to accompany him on his new expedition, Henson readily agreed. They sailed from the port of Brooklyn, New York, in June 6, 1891, and reached their final destination, McCormick Bay, in Greenland, more than three weeks later.

Henson immediately went to work, constructing a house at the campsite and building sledges—large sleds—to carry the expedition farther north. Henson learned many skills from the Eskimos who visited the campsite, including how to handle a sledge and dog team, and he taught these skills to Peary.

Following the return to New York of the Peary expedition in September 1892, Henson spent several months recovering from an eye injury he had received in Greenland. He then accompanied Peary on a lecture tour to raise money for another trip to the Arctic. Their second trip began in the summer of 1893 and continued for more than two years. Again Henson was an invaluable companion, assisting Peary in his explorations, frequently saving him from near disaster, and helping him to retrieve two large meteorites.

Shortly after their return in September 1895, Henson was hired by the American Museum of Natural History in New York City to help set up an exhibition of animal specimens that the men had brought back from the Arctic. Henson made two more brief trips to Greenland with Peary in 1896 and 1897 to secure a giant meteorite that had to be left behind in 1895. On the second mission they brought back the 35-ton object to the American Museum, where it is still on display.

In January 1897 Peary, who was now a famous figure, publicly announced his intention of reaching the North Pole. The following year Henson accompanied Peary on a four year expedition to the Arctic.

Despite many attempts, however, they were unable to reach their goal because of hazardous weather conditions. After their return in the fall of 1902, Peary told Henson that it would be several years before he could raise enough money to mount another expedition to the Arctic. Henson took a break from polar exploration and became a porter on the Pennsylvania Railroad, traveling throughout the country for three years.

In the summer of 1905 Henson was summoned back to New York by Peary, who was now ready to embark on another expedition, this time in a boat made especially strong to move through the frozen northern seas. The boat was named the *Roosevelt*, after President Theodore Roosevelt, one of Peary's strongest supporters. Much of the preparatory work for this expedition was done by Henson. This time they got within 175 miles of the North Pole, but the men had to turn back because of poor weather conditions, the loss of many of their sled dogs, and a dwindling supply of food.

In 1907, during preparations for the return journey, Henson married Lucy Ross, a young woman he had met two years earlier in New York. Less than a year later, in July 1908, he was back on board the *Roosevelt*, sailing with Peary for what was to be a final journey northward.

Finally, after months of backbreaking preparation, Peary, Henson, and four Eskimos set out by sledge on the last leg of the journey on April 1, 1909. Henson himself was responsible for breaking the trail through the snow and ice. Six days later they had achieved their goal: all six men had reached the North Pole.

When Peary and Henson returned to the United States that summer, they expected to be feted for their discovery. Instead, they discovered that Dr. Frederick Cook, a physician who had accompanied Peary and Henson on their 1891 trip to the Arctic, claimed that he had reached the North Pole the previous year. Cook's story had already been accepted by the general public, and there was little celebration for Peary, an arrogant man who could easily offend others. As for Henson, he was dismissed as "an ignorant negro" who had probably caused Peary to mistake his location. While asserting that he had indeed reached the North Pole, Peary made no attempt to defend the accomplishments of Henson, and a rift grew between the two men.

By 1910 Cook's claim was shown to be false and Peary was generally acknowledged as the conqueror of the North Pole. Numerous honors were showered on him, and he was promoted to the rank of admiral in the U.S. Navy. Henson, however, was quickly forgotten and took a job parking cars in a garage. In 1912 he published an account of his adventures, *A Negro Explorer at the North Pole*, but it was not popular.

In 1913, through the efforts of a black politician in New York City, Henson was given a job as a messenger in the U.S. Customs Bureau. He was later promoted to clerk and worked at this job until his retirement in 1940, on a pension of $1,020 a year—

a pittance compared with the enormous pension granted to Peary before his death in 1920.

Not everyone had forgotten Henson, however. As the decades passed, black organizations mounted campaigns to win recognition for him. In 1937 Henson was finally admitted to the Explorers Club, and eight years later—36 years after the discovery of the North Pole—he received a medal from the U.S. Navy. In 1954 he and his wife were invited to the White House by President Dwight D. Eisenhower. Henson died less than a year later, on March 9, 1955, in New York City.

ERNEST EVERETT JUST

Zoologist Ernest Everett Just was born in Charleston, South Carolina, on August 14, 1883, the third child of Charles and Mary Just. Ernest's father was a construction worker at the Charleston docks, and his mother worked as a seamstress. Before Ernest was a year old, his older brother and sister died. Within several years his mother had given birth to another son, Hunter, and a daughter, Inez.

When Ernest Just was four years old, further tragedy struck the family. Both his father and grandfather died, and his mother was now the sole support of herself and her three small children. For a while she taught school in Charleston and worked as a miner on nearby James Island. With other African Americans, Mary Just later founded a new town on the island, which was named Maryville in her honor.

Mary Just ran the local school in Maryville, and Ernest attended classes there. During his years on the island he also had to do household chores and help care for his younger brother and sister, but during what little free time he had, Ernest liked to explore the island and investigate the plants and animals that lived there. When he was 13, his mother raised enough money to send him to an all-black boarding school in Orangeburg, South Carolina, to prepare him for a teaching career. When Ernest finished his studies there three years later, he returned home because his mother thought he was not yet old enough to become a teacher.

Believing that her son should get further education, Mary Just tried to find another school for him. In a church newspaper she read about Kimball Union Academy, an institution in Meriden, New Hampshire, sponsored by a religious organization called the Christian Endeavor World Unity Group. According to the article, Kimball Union offered scholarships to exceptional students. She wrote to them about Ernest, but before they received a reply, Ernest decided to visit the school.

There was no money for the trip, so Ernest found a job on a small ship sailing from Charleston to New York. He was paid five dollars when the ship docked in New York. To earn enough money for a train ticket to New Hampshire, he worked for a month as a cook in a New York restaurant. When he finally arrived at Kimball Union, he discovered that he had won a scholarship to the school.

Ernest Just completed Kimball Union's four-year program in three years and graduated in 1903 as the top student—and the only black—in his class. He was now on his own, for his mother had died the year before and relatives were caring for his brother and sister. He received a scholarship to Dartmouth College, where he first studied classical languages and literature. In his second year, Just became increasingly interested in science, especially biology. He was encouraged in his studies by his biology teacher, William Patten, who later became a close friend.

In his junior year, Just was named a Rufus Choate Scholar, the highest award offered by the college. He graduated with high honors in 1907 and was elected to Phi Beta Kappa, the national honor society. Just had decided that he wanted to pursue a career as a research biologist, specializing in the study of small marine animals like sandworms and starfish. However, there were few opportunities in this field for young black men. He took a job teaching biology at Howard University, an all-black institution in Washington, D.C., and tried to do research at the university laboratory. However, the laboratory equipment was inadequate for his experiments, and after he was made head of the department in 1908 he found that he had little time for independent research.

In 1909 Just's former professor and friend William Patten introduced him to Frank R. Lillie, who was the chairman of the biology department at the University of Chicago. Lillie was also the head of the Marine Biological Laboratory at Woods Hole, Massachusetts. Known as Woods Hole, the facility was a famous research center where scientists gathered every summer to do research.

Lillie invited Just to spend the summer of 1909 at Woods Hole as his research assistant. Impressed with Just's work, Lillie invited him back the following summer, and soon afterward Just's work was respected to such an extent that he returned to Woods Hole each summer as an equal participant with other distinguished scientists. In 1912 he published his first research report, an account of the early moments of a sandworm's life. Just became an authority on the embryology of marine animals and published many studies about them.

That same year, in June, he married Ethel Highwarden after a long courtship. Ethel was a teacher of German in the College of Arts and Sciences at Howard. After planning a trip to Europe, the highlight being Germany, where they were both anxious to visit, Ethel gave up her honeymoon so her husband could get on with his career. The couple had three children: Margaret, Highwarden, and Maribel, born in 1913, 1917, and 1922. Even after the marriage broke up, Just attempted to maintain a relationship with his children. His oldest and favorite child, Margaret, accompanied him on his first trip to Europe.

Lillie encouraged Just to work for an advanced degree in biology, and in 1915 he took a leave of absence from Howard and enrolled as a graduate student at the University of Chicago. In one year he completed all requirements for a doctoral degree and received a Ph.D. with high honors in 1916. Even before beginning his graduate studies, Just had become widely known as an outstanding scientist through his research at Woods Hole. In 1915 the NAACP (National Association for the Advancement of Colored People) awarded Just the first Spingarn Medal, given annually to an outstanding black American.

Despite his prominence, Just was unable to get an appointment at a major American university that would allow him time to do research as well as teach. He was married and had a family to support, so he continued teaching classes at Howard University while supporting his research with small grants from major philanthropic foundations.

By the 1920s Just was an internationally known biologist. Because he had a thorough knowledge of French and German, he was able to keep abreast of the work of European scientists in his field and to participate fully in foreign conferences.

The fact that he was treated with more respect abroad than he was in the United States gradually embittered Just. He stopped going to Woods Hole and began spending more time abroad doing research, first at a laboratory in Naples, Italy, and during the early 1930s at the Kaiser Wilhelm Institute in Berlin. He continued to teach part-time at Howard but became increasingly reluctant to encourage black students to receive advanced training. He believed that they would only be frustrated in their attempts to pursue scientific careers because of strong racial prejudice in the United States.

By the mid-1930s Just was doing most of his research at the Sorbonne in Paris. During this time he wrote his best-known work, *The Biology of the Cell Surface*, which was published in 1939. During his lifetime Just published about 60 scientific papers as well as a monograph, *Basic Methods for Experiments on Eggs of Marine Animals*, which also appeared in 1939.

Just had settled permanently in France in the late 1930s and now considered it his home country. However, World War II began in the fall of 1939 and Germany invaded France the following spring. Just offered himself for military service, but the French government turned him down; when France surrendered to Germany, he was imprisoned for a short time. Since the United States was not yet at war with Germany, U.S. government officials were able to free him from prison. However, he had been in poor health for some time, and his prison stay only aggravated his condition.

Just had divorced his wife, Ethel, and remarried Maid Hedwig Schnetzler, with whom he had a daughter, Elisabeth. In the fall of 1940 Just returned to Washington, D.C. Suffering from cancer, his health grew worse and he was unable to pursue further research. He died in Washington on October 27, 1941. Just's pioneering research in embryology and cytology (the study of cells) was the basis for later important studies in genetics and the mechanism of heredity.

LEWIS LATIMER

Inventor Lewis Latimer was born on September 4, 1848, in Chelsea, Massachusetts, a small town near Boston. He was the fourth child of George and Rebecca Latimer, who were former slaves. Lewis's paternal grandfather, Mitchell Latimer, had been a wealthy plantation owner and slaveholder in Norfolk, Virginia, in the early 19th century and had sired Lewis's father, George, with one of his slaves.

In 1842 George Latimer and his wife, Rebecca, fled slavery for the safety of Massachusetts, which had banned the selling and owning of slaves some years earlier. They were immediately hunted down as fugitive slaves by their owners, and New England's leading abolitionists—including orator Frederick Douglass and William Lloyd Garrison, editor of *The Liberator*, an antislavery newspaper—fought to keep them from being sent back to Virginia, where they faced imprisonment and possible execution. Funds were quickly raised to purchase George Latimer from his owner—Rebecca had eluded capture—and the couple were reunited in time for the birth of their first child, George junior.

Although George Latimer, Sr., had become a celebrity, earning a living in the North was difficult for him. After the passage of the Fugitive Slave Law of 1850, his life became even more filled with hardship. Although his freedom had been paid for, at any time he might be seized and returned to slavery because, according to the act, any white man could claim ownership of any black simply by swearing that the black had once been his lawful property and had run away; blacks had no legal rights, and their written and verbal claims meant nothing against the sworn testimony of a white man.

George Latimer avoided seizure by moving frequently with his wife and four small children. During the 1850s he ran a barbershop in a black neighborhood of Boston, assisted by young Lewis. Constant worry about his safety preyed on George Latimer, especially after he learned of the famous March 1857 decision by the U.S. Supreme Court to return fugitive slave Dred Scott to his former owner in Missouri. In 1858 George Latimer suddenly disappeared; family and friends assumed that fear of recapture had led him to desert his family. Lewis Latimer did not hear from his father again until many years later.

Lewis and his two older brothers and sister helped his mother support the family. During the Civil War, Lewis lied about his age so that he could fight with the Union against slavery. He served as a seaman aboard a U.S. Navy gunboat that participated in a blockade of southern ports during the final year of the war. Following his discharge in July 1865, Latimer returned to Boston and lived with his mother.

Although jobs for both blacks and whites were scarce, Latimer found employment as an office boy with Crosby and Gould, a firm of patent lawyers. They employed artists who made sketches of inventions—a drawing of an invention had to be submitted to the U.S. government when the inventor applied for a patent. Latimer had a natural aptitude for drawing, and he was eager to learn this trade. While he performed his office duties, he carefully observed the work of the staff artists. From his small salary he saved enough money to buy the instruction books and drawing tools, and at home each night he taught himself basic draftsmanship. After several months, Latimer approached the head draftsman, showed him his work, and was soon allowed to do simple sketches. Latimer eventually rose to become head draftsman at Crosby and Gould.

As he sketched other men's inventions, Latimer began working on some ideas of his own. In February 1874, along with his associate W. C. Brown, Latimer proudly received his first patent—for an improved water closet, or toilet, used on passenger trains. Two years later Latimer participated in a history-making event when he helped Alexander Graham Bell prepare his patent application for a brand new invention, the telephone. Latimer not only executed the drawings of the device but is also believed to have helped Bell with the written description that accompanied the drawings.

Latimer remained at Crosby and Gould for several more years, then worked briefly for another patent lawyer and as a pattern drawer at an iron foundry. In 1879 Latimer and his wife, Mary, whom he had married six years earlier, moved to Bridgeport, Connecticut, where his sister, Margaret, and her husband lived. He worked for a while as a paperhanger, then found work as a draftsman in a machine shop. One day Hiram Maxim, an inventor who owned the U.S. Electric Lighting Company, stopped by the shop. He was impressed by Latimer and promptly hired him to work at his own company as a draftsman. As he made his drawings, Latimer also taught himself everything he could learn about electrical lighting.

A year earlier, Thomas A. Edison had received a patent for an electric light bulb, and there was a growing demand from both businesses and private home owners for electrical lighting. Edison's bulb was not long-lasting, however; the filament, or wire, inside the glass produced light by being heated until it glowed, but filaments burned out after only a few days at most, and then the entire bulb had to be replaced.

Maxim, Edison, and other inventors were trying to create longer-lasting filaments, and Latimer decided that he, too, would make an attempt. After much trial and error, he invented a long-lasting carbon filament that was cheap to produce—and revolutionized the field of electric lighting. He received a patent for the device, but the credit for its invention—and all the profits—went to Hiram Maxim and the U.S. Electric Lighting Company.

Latimer, perhaps realizing that it would be futile to seek proper recognition, continued to work on improvements in electric lighting devices at Maxim's firm. Just a few months after patenting his process for making carbon filaments, Latimer and an associate, John Tregoning, received another patent, this time for an electric arc lamp, a device that did not use a filament.

Latimer soon became recognized as an expert in the electric light industry, and he acted as a consultant in the construction of the first electric plants in Philadelphia, Montreal, and New York City. He also supervised the installation of lights and wiring in public and private facilities in those three cities. His accomplishments in Montreal were especially impressive, since he had to direct a crew of workmen who spoke only

French. Latimer taught himself the language in order to write specific technical directions for the workmen; later he taught himself German, too.

In the spring of 1882 Maxim sent Latimer to England to open a new light bulb factory, but when Latimer returned to the United States several months later, he discovered that his job had been eliminated. About this time, Hiram Maxim wrote his autobiography, taking credit for perfecting the light bulb but not mentioning Lewis Latimer.

For a few months Latimer worked for an electric lighting company in Brooklyn. Then he was hired by Maxim's archrival, Thomas Edison, who worked out of offices in New York City and laboratories in New Jersey. Latimer was put in charge of the company library, and he had the additional duties of collecting information for use in lawsuits to protect Edison's numerous patents. (During his lifetime, Edison received nearly 1,100 patents for various devices, including the phonograph, the microphone, and picture photography.)

During the years that he worked for Edison, Latimer patented other devices of his own invention, including a combination cooling-disinfecting apparatus (the forerunner of a window air conditioner) and a locking coat and hatrack. With encouragement from Edison, Latimer wrote a book, *Incandescent Electric Lighting, A Practical Description of the Edison System*, which was published in 1890. In his spare time he painted and wrote poetry. He also became a strong supporter of equal rights for black Americans and corresponded with black leaders Frederick Douglass and Booker T. Washington.

From 1896 to 1911 Latimer served as chief draftsman of the Board of Patent Control, an organization formed jointly by Edison's organization, now called the General Electric Company, and its chief rival, the Westinghouse Company, to avoid costly legal battles between the two companies over patent rights. After the board was abolished in 1911, Latimer became a patent consultant for an engineering firm headed by Edwin Hammer. He retired in 1922 because of failing eyesight but received a generous pension from the General Electric Company. Four years earlier Latimer's contributions to General Electric had been officially recognized when he was named a member of the Edison Pioneers, 28 individuals who had been the founders of Edison's company.

Latimer died on December 11, 1928. Nearly 50 years later, during the 1970s, his contributions to science and industry were rediscovered and widely acknowledged. In 1982 a street in Flushing, New York, the community where he lived for many years, was named after him. Six years later, Latimer's house was saved from demolition and moved to a new site, where it will be reopened in 1995 as a museum.

❧ FURTHER READING ❧

Benjamin Banneker

Bedini, Silvio A. *The Life of Benjamin Banneker*. New York: Scribners, 1971.

Conley, Kevin. *Benjamin Banneker*. New York: Chelsea House, 1989.

Ferris, Jeri. *What Are You Figuring Now? A Story About Benjamin Banneker*. Minneapolis: Carolrhoda, 1988.

James Beckwourth

Beckwourth, James P., and T. D. Bonner. *The Life and Adventures of James P. Beckwourth, Mountaineer, Scout, Pioneer, and Chief of the Crow Nation*. 1856. Reprint. Lincoln: University of Nebraska Press, 1972.

Dolan, Sean. *James Beckwourth*. New York: Chelsea House, 1992.

Wilson, Elinor. *Jim Beckwourth: Black Mountain Man, War Chief of the Crows, Trader, Trapper, Explorer, Frontiersman, Guide, Scout, Interpreter, Adventurer, and Gaudy Liar*. Norman: University of Oklahoma Press, 1972.

Guion Bluford

Haskins, James, and Kathleen Benson. *Space Challenger: The Story of Guion Bluford*. Minneapolis: Carolrhoda Books, 1984.

George Washington Carver

Adair, Gene. *George Washington Carver*. New York: Chelsea House, 1989.

Kremer, Gary R. *George Washington Carver: In His Own Words*. Columbia: University of Missouri Press, 1986.

McMurry, Linda O. *George Washington Carver: Scientist and Symbol*. New York: Oxford Unversity Press, 1981.

Charles Drew

Lichello, Robert. *Pioneer in Blood Plasma: Dr. Charles Richard Drew*. New York: Simon & Schuster, 1968.

Mahone-Lonesome, Robyn. *Charles Drew*. New York: Chelsea House, 1990.

Wynes, Charles E. *Charles Richard Drew: The Man and the Myth*. Urbana: University of Illinois Press, 1988.

Matthew Henson

Dolan, Edward F. *Matthew Henson, Black Explorer*. New York: Dodd, Mead, 1979.

Gilman, Michael. *Matthew Henson*. New York: Chelsea House, 1988.

Robinson, Bradley, with Matthew Henson. *Dark Companion*. New York: McBride, 1947.

Ernest Everett Just

Manning, Kenneth R. *Black Apollo of Science*. New York: Oxford University Press, 1983.

Lewis Latimer

Norman, Winifred Latimer, and Lily Patterson. *Lewis Latimer*. New York: Chelsea House, 1994.

Turner, Glennette Tilley. *Lewis Howard Latimer*. Englewood Cliffs, NJ: Silver Burdett, 1991.

PICTURE CREDITS

RICHARD RENNERT has edited the nearly 100 volumes in Chelsea House's award-winning BLACK AMERICANS OF ACHIEVEMENT series, which tells the stories of black men and women who have helped shape the course of modern history. He is also the author of several sports biographies, including *Henry Aaron*, *Jesse Owens*, and *Jackie Robinson*. He is a graduate of Haverford College in Haverford, Pennsylvania.